PENNYWHISTLE *Listen & Learn*
HOMESPUN MUSIC INSTRUCTION

Cathal McCONNELL
TEACHES
Irish Pennywhistle

A Hands-on Course
in Traditional Irish
Repertoire and Technique
*Featuring a Comprehensive
Audio Lesson on CD*

T0045369

Cover Photo by Happy Traum

Audio Editor: George James

Mastered by: Ted Orr at
Nevessa Productions, Woodstock, N.Y.

ISBN 0-7935-6254-6

HOMESPUN®
Tapes

HAL•LEONARD®
CORPORATION
7777 W. BLUEMOUND RD. P.O. BOX 13819 MILWAUKEE, WI 53213

CD instruction makes it easy! Find the section of the lesson you want with the press of a finger; play that segment over and over until you've mastered it; easily skip over parts you've already mastered—no clumsy rewinding or fast-forwarding to find your spot; listen with the best possible audio fidelity; follow along track-by-track with the book.

Table of Contents

This book contains music examples and all of the instructional songs from the CD, and are labeled with track icons (◆) for the ease of locating the corresponding tracks. The remaining tracks listed here contain detailed explanation and instruction for these songs.

Cathal McConnell, Master of the Whistle

Cathal McConnell is best known through his long-time association with the Boys of the Lough, one of the finest traditional music groups to ever come out of the British Isles. A co-founder of the band and a member for nearly thirty years, Cathal and the Boys have performed in major concert halls throughout the world and have recorded nearly twenty albums.

Cathal comes from a family of flute players. Born in Co. Fermanagh, in Northern Ireland, he won All-Ireland Championships in both flute and tin whistle in 1962, at the age of 18. Five years later he started touring with the first incarnation of the Boys of the Lough and has been with them ever since as instrumentalist and lead singer.

Comprised of members from various parts of the British Isles (Northumberland, the Shetland Islands, Scotland and Ireland), the Boys of the Lough are masters of Celtic musical traditions. Like that other long-running act, the Chieftains, their music blends impeccable technique and sensitivity with very tight ensemble playing. The overall feeling of their performances is of a group of skilled, well-integrated musicians playing together for the pure pleasure of it.

Cathal has become well known over the years as a true virtuoso of the flute and pennywhistle. He brings his years of expertise to this wonderful introduction to a true folk instrument.

The pennywhistle is a small, high-pitched whistle flute which is end-blown like a recorder. Also known as a tin whistle, it is usually made of metal, with six finger holes and a mouthpiece. They are available in a number of different keys. All of the music contained on the CD and in this book is for the D pennywhistle.

◆4 D Major Scale

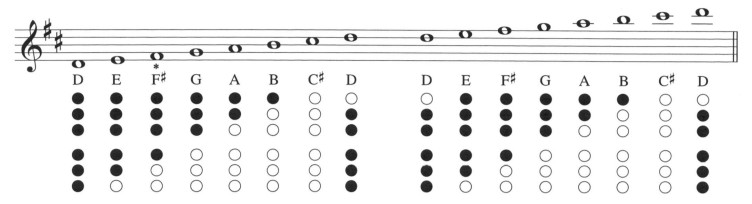

| D | E | F♯* | G | A | B | C♯ | D | D | E | F♯ | G | A | B | C♯ | D |

*Due to the nature of the instrument, the pennywhistle being designed to play in specific keys, Cathal references all sharped notes by their natural name on the CD.

◆5 It's Not Yet Day
(Neil Shay Na Law)
(in D)

Slow Air

◆6 G Major Scale

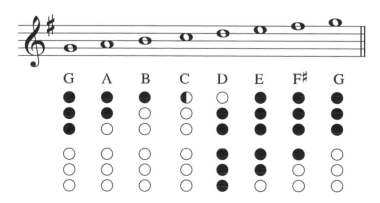

| G | A | B | C | D | E | F♯ | G |

⑦ O'Donnell Abú
(in D)

9 *Sí Beag Sí Mór*
(in D)

◆12 The South Wind

(in G)

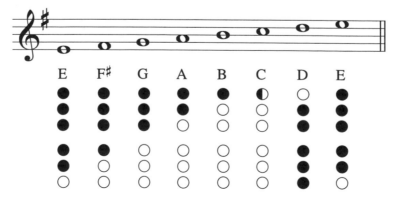

◆14 E Minor Scale

15 The King of the Faeries
(in E minor)

16 A Minor Scale

⬥18 Brian Bohru's March
(in A minor)

20 A Major Scale

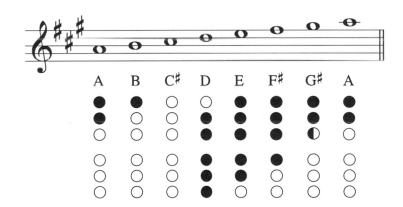

21 The Lakes of Ponchartrain

(in A)

22 The Little Beggarman
(in A)

24 **B Minor Scale**

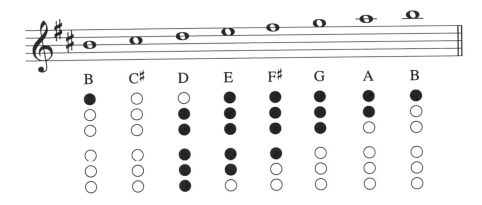

25 **The Foggy Dew**

(in B minor)

Rolls

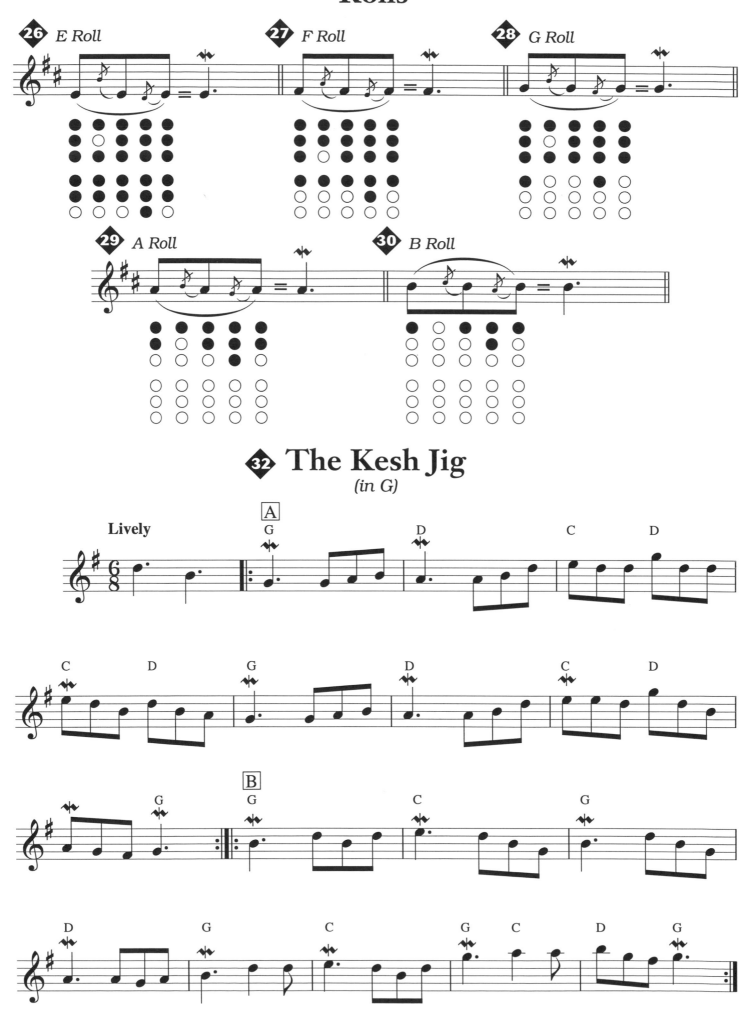

🔷35 The Temperance Reel
(in G)

36 Give Me Your Hand

(in G)

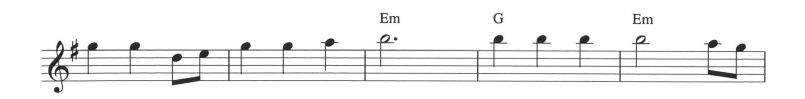

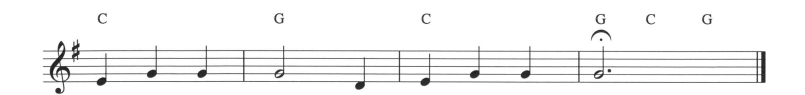

A Selected Discography

Date	Title	European Release	US Release

Cathal McConnell with
The Boys of the Lough:

Date	Title	European Release	US Release
1972	*The Boys of the Lough*	Trailer LER2028	Shanachie 79002
1973	*Second Album*	Trailer LER2090	Rounder 3006
1975	*Live at Passim's*	Transatlantic TRA296	Philo PH1026
1976	*Lochaber No More*	Transatlantic TRA311	Philo PH1031
1976	*The Piper's Broken Finger*	Transatlantic TRA333	Philo PH1042
1977	*Good Friends–Good Music*	Transatlantic TRA354	Philo PH1051
1978	*Wish You Were Here*	Transatlantic TRA359	Flying Fish FF070
1980	*Regrouped*	Topic 12TS409	Flying Fish FF225
1981	*In the Tradition*	Topic 12TS422	Flying Fish FF263
1983	*Open Road*	Topic 12TS433	Flying Fish FF310
1985	*To Welcome Paddy Home*	Lough 001	Shanachie 79061
1986	*Far From Home*	AUK 001	Shanachie 79065
1987	*Farewell and Remember Me*	Lough 002	Shanachie 79067
1988	*Sweet Rural Shade*	Lough 003	Shanachie 79068
1992	*Live at Carnegie Hall*	Lough 004	Sage Arts 0301
1992	*The Fair Hills of Ireland*	Lough 005	Sage Arts 0302

Cathal McConnell and Robin Morton:

Date	Title	European Release	US Release
1969	*An Irish Jubilee*	Ossian, OSS24 (reissue)	

LISTEN & LEARN SERIES

This exciting new series features lessons from the top pros with in-depth CD instruction and thorough accompanying book.

GUITAR

**Russ Barenberg Teaches
Twenty Bluegrass Guitar Solos**
00695220 Book/CD Pack.................................$19.95

**Keola Beamer Teaches
Hawaiian Slack Key Guitar**
00695338 Book/CD Pack.................................$19.95

**Rory Block Teaches Classics
of Country Blues Guitar**
00699065 Book/CD Pack.................................$19.95

**Dan Crary Teaches Guitar
Flatpicking Repertoire**
00695363 Book/CD Pack.................................$19.95

**Cathy Fink and Marcy Marxer's
Kids' Guitar Songbook**
00695258 Book/CD Pack.................................$14.95

The Guitar of Jorma Kaukonen
00695184 Book/CD Pack.................................$19.95

**Tony Rice Teaches
Bluegrass Guitar**
00695045 Book/CD Pack.................................$19.95

**Artie Traum Teaches
Essential Chords & Progressions
for Acoustic Guitar**
00695259 Book/CD Pack.................................$14.95

**Artie Traum Teaches 101
Essential Riffs for Acoustic Guitar**
00695260 Book/CD Pack.................................$14.95

**Happy Traum Teaches
Blues Guitar**
00841082 Book/CD Pack.................................$19.95

**Richard Thompson Teaches
Traditional Guitar Instrumentals**
00841083 Book/CD Pack.................................$19.95

BANJO

**Tony Trischka Teaches
20 Easy Banjo Solos**
00699056 Book/CD Pack.................................$19.95

MANDOLIN

**Sam Bush Teaches Bluegrass
Mandolin Repertoire**
00695339 Book/CD Pack.................................$19.95

HARMONICA

**Paul Butterfield Teaches
Blues Harmonica**
00699089 Book/CD Pack.................................$19.95

**John Sebastian Teaches
Blues Harmonica**
00841074 Book/CD Pack.................................$19.95

FOR MORE INFORMATION, SEE YOUR LOCAL MUSIC DEALER,
OR WRITE TO:

HAL•LEONARD® CORPORATION

7777 W. BLUEMOUND RD. P.O. BOX 13819 MILWAUKEE, WI 53213

PIANO

**David Bennett Cohen
Teaches Blues Piano**
A Hands-On Course in Traditional Blues Piano
00841084 Volume 1 Book/CD Pack..................$19.95
00290498 Volume 2 Book/CD Pack..................$19.95

**Warren Bernhardt
Teaches Jazz Piano**
*Volume 1 – A Hands-On Course
in Improvisation and Technique*
00699062 Volume 1 Book/CD Pack................$19.95

Volume 2 – Creating Harmony and Building Solos
00699084 Volume 2 Book/CD Pack................$19.95

**Dr. John Teaches
New Orleans Piano**
*Volume 1 – In-Depth Sessions with a
Master Musician*
00699090 Book/CD Pack.............................$19.95

Volume 2 – Building a Blues Repertoire
00699093 Book/CD Pack.............................$19.95

Volume 3 – Sanctifying the Blues
00699094 Book/CD Pack.............................$19.95

PENNYWHISTLE

**Cathal McConnell Teaches
Irish Pennywhistle**
00841081 Book/CD Pack.................................$19.95

0199